Snooze-O-Rama

The Strange Ways That Animals Sleep

For Abby & Jack ... and sleepyheads everywhere
—M.B.

To Omi and Mia, many thanks
—K.R.

ACKNOWLEDGEMENTS Sincere thanks to my editor, Kendra Brown, for your genuine enthusiasm and ten years (and counting!) of editing expertise. I'm grateful to Kyle Reed for your wonderful artwork, as well as designer Alisa Baldwin for your talented eye. Thank you to the amazing team at Owlkids Books for all you do. Many thanks to Karen Li for taking my kernel of an idea and transforming it just like that. And, as always, thank you to Sam and Grace, who learned the true value of sleeping in ... eventually.

Owlkids Books acknowledges the financial support of the Canada Council for the Arts, the Ontario Arts Council, the Government of Canada through the Canada Book Fund (CBF) and the Government of Ontario through the Ontario Creates Book Initiative for our publishing activities.

Published in Canada by Owlkids Books Inc., 1 Eglinton Avenue East, Toronto, ON M4P 3A1
Published in the US by Owlkids Books Inc., 1700 Fourth Street, Berkeley, CA 94710

Library of Congress Control Number: 2020939445

Library and Archives Canada Cataloguing in Publication

Title: Snooze-o-rama : the strange ways that animals sleep / written by Maria Birmingham ;
illustrated by Kyle Reed.
Other titles: Strange ways that animals sleep
Names: Birmingham, Maria, author. | Reed, Kyle, illustrator.
Description: Includes bibliographical references.
Identifiers: Canadiana 20200259067 | ISBN 9781771474047 (hardcover)
Subjects: LCSH: Bedtime—Juvenile literature. | LCSH: Sleep behavior in animals—Juvenile literature.
Classification: LCC HQ784.B43 B57 2021 | DDC j649/.6—dc23

Edited by Kendra Brown | Designed by Alisa Baldwin

Manufactured in Guangdong Province, Dongguan City, China, in September 2020,
by Toppan Leefung Packaging & Printing (Dongguan) Co., Ltd. Job #BAYDC83

A   B   C   D   E   F

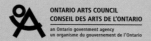
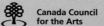
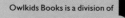
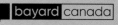
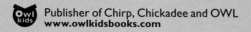

ONTARIO ARTS COUNCIL
CONSEIL DES ARTS DE L'ONTARIO
an Ontario government agency
un organisme du gouvernement de l'Ontario

Canada Council
for the Arts
Conseil des Arts
du Canada

Canada

Publisher of Chirp, Chickadee and OWL
www.owlkidsbooks.com

Owlkids Books is a division of bayard canada

Snooze-O-Rama

The Strange Ways That Animals Sleep

Written by
MARIA BIRMINGHAM

Illustrated by
KYLE REED

Owlkids Books

Shh!

It's time to quiet down. The animals in this book are ready for a rest. Like you, they need to sleep. And each one sleeps in its own way. So curl up, get comfy, and yawn if you must. Come along with these tired beasts as they settle down to snooze.

While you cover yourself with a blanket ...

... an otter wraps itself in seaweed.

A sea otter falls asleep while floating on its back. Sometimes it wraps itself in strands of seaweed. They act like a boat anchor, keeping the otter from drifting away. Several otters may head to slumberville together, each one wrapped in its own seaweed anchor.

While you doze off during a long trip ...

... a frigate bird nods off as it soars.

The frigate bird can fly for up to two months without ever coming in for a landing. That means it has to sleep in the sky! The bird sneaks short naps that last just ten seconds each. It often snoozes with one eye open, but sometimes it nods off with both eyes closed.

While you pull on your pj's ...

... a parrotfish snuggles up in slime.

Every time it's ready to sleep, the parrotfish burps up a slimy substance and covers itself from head to tail. This goop is like its own special sleeping bag! The clear cocoon keeps tiny bloodsucking parasites from nibbling on the parrotfish while it snoozes. It may also protect the fish from predators by masking its scent.

While you hug your favorite stuffy ...

... a bee grips tight to a nearby plant.

At nighttime, bees go from buzzzz to zzzz. While many bees return to their nests to rest, cuckoo bees often settle down to sleep on plants. The bugs use their strong jaws to bite into stems or leaves. They slumber there all night long, hanging on with nothing but their mouths.

While you make your bed each morning ...

... an orangutan builds its bed each night.

Every night, the orangutan climbs high into the treetops. There, it gathers thick branches and weaves them together to create a nest. The great ape then adds a layer of twigs to make a comfy mattress to sleep on. Sometimes it even uses a leafy branch as a blanket or forms a pillow from a pile of leaves.

While you and your family fall asleep
under the stars ...

... a group of whales snoozes under the sea.

For a long time, it was a mystery how sperm whales slept in the deep blue. Now we know the huge mammals gather in a pod to doze near the surface. They bob and drift in one spot with their heads pointing up and their tails pointing down—almost as if they are standing.

While you climb onto the bunk above ...

... an oxpecker naps beneath a giraffe.

The yellow-billed oxpecker spends its days perched atop a giraffe, picking through its towering friend's hair looking for bugs to eat. Come nighttime, it finds the perfect place to rest: in the giraffe's armpit! It grips on tight with its claws, snoozing all night long. By sleeping there, the oxpecker is guaranteed to find a buggy breakfast when it wakes.

While you drift off as you read ...

... an ant falls asleep as it works.

There's a lot of work to get done in a fire ant colony. That means there's not much time to sleep. To get through the day and night, worker ants take short naps. The little bugs nod off up to 250 times each day! Most of their naps are just one minute long.

While you sleep late on the weekend ...

... a turtle slumbers all winter long.

In wintertime, painted turtles dig into the muddy bottom of ponds, lakes, and rivers. As the water at the surface freezes, the turtles fall into a deep sleep that lasts for months. When the cold water around them warms up, the turtles sense that spring has sprung. They wake up and get back to doing the things turtles do!

While you turn off your light
for the night ...

... a bat is just waking up.

A fruit bat spends its days sleeping away. It dangles upside down from a branch, hanging on by its feet. The bat even wraps its wings around itself like a cozy blanket. As night falls, this furry flyer wakes up and searches the dark for food. Come sunrise, it'll head back to the treetops for another day of dozing.

While you get comfy
on a pillow ...

... a walrus rests on its pouches.

Sometimes this plump marine mammal drifts off to sleep while floating in the ocean. In its throat, the walrus has special pouches that hold air. They act like a life jacket, keeping the walrus's head out of the water so it can peacefully snooze as it glides along.

And while you pile into your
parents' bed …

... a meerkat family sleeps in a heap.

Meerkats live in large groups called mobs. A mob works as a team to hunt, raise pups, and watch for danger. So it's no surprise that meerkats stick together at bedtime, too. They cram into a furry pile in their burrow, with adult females squishing into the middle of the mound. Sleep tight!

Who knew there were so many different ways to sleep?

All this talk of sleep may have you wondering why you need to rest at all. Sleep is important for you, just as it is for many animals. It gives the body time to relax after a busy day. It also lets your brain sort through everything that happened to you while you were awake.

You need about ten hours of sleep each night to keep your body and brain healthy. But how much do animals need? It depends. Some, like the giraffe and the African elephant, get by with only two hours of sleep a day. Others pretty much snore their lives away. The giant armadillo, for example, stays awake for just six hours. That means this sleepyhead settles into its burrow for an eighteen-hour rest every day. Imagine that!

And now, it's time to leave all these animals to snuggle and sleep in their favorite spots. But first, do tell— where is *your* favorite place to snooze?

SUGGESTED READING

BARMAN, ADRIENNE. *Creaturepedia: Welcome to the Greatest Show on Earth.* London: Wide-Eyed Editions, 2015.

BROWN, MARTIN. *Lesser Spotted Animals.* London: Scholastic Inc., 2016.

CASSANY, MIA. *Wilderness: Earth's Amazing Habitats.* New York: Prestel Junior, 2019.

DAVIES, NICOLA. *Many: The Diversity of Life on Earth.* Somerville: Candlewick, 2017.

HAWKINS, EMILY AND RACHEL WILLIAMS. *Atlas of Animal Adventures: A Collection of Nature's Most Unmissable Events, Epic Migrations and Extraordinary Behaviours.* London: Wide-Eyed Editions, 2016.

HOARE, BEN. *An Anthology of Intriguing Animals.* London: DK, 2018.

JUDGE, LITA. *Homes in the Wild: Where Baby Animals and Their Parents Live.* New York: Roaring Brook Press, 2019.

National Geographic Kids. Online.

POON, ANNA. *World's Wackiest Animals: 100 Uncommonly Peculiar Creatures.* Melbourne: Lonely Planet Kids, 2020.

SÄFSTRÖM, MAJA. *The Illustrated Compendium of Amazing Animal Facts.* Berkeley: Ten Speed Press, 2016.

San Diego Zoo. Online.

WWF Go Wild. Online.